HOMEMADE LOW-CARB LIFESTYLE

by Veronika Slavik
Holistic Low Carb Health Coach

© 2025 Veronika Slavik

First published in 2024.

This revised edition published in 2025.

This edition includes a redesigned cover, updated images, refined page design, and minor improvements to selected recipes for accuracy and clarity. The core content remains unchanged.

All rights reserved. No part of this cookbook may be reproduced, distributed, or transmitted in any form or by any means, including photocopying, recording, or other electronic or mechanical methods, except for brief quotations embodied in critical reviews and specific noncommercial uses permitted by copyright law.

The recipes, photographs, and text contained in this cookbook are the sole property of Veronika Slavik and are protected under international copyright laws. Any unauthorised use, reproduction, or distribution of these materials is strictly prohibited and may result in legal action.

Every effort has been made to ensure the accuracy of the information presented in this cookbook. However, neither Veronika Slavik nor the publisher can be held responsible for any errors or omissions that may occur.

All trademarks mentioned in this cookbook belong to their respective owners.

ISBN: 9798320964799

Imprint: Independently published

Contents

01 Introductions
02 Health Tips
03 BREAKFAST AND BRUNCH RECIPES 6
04 SOUP 15
05 LUNCH RECIPES 21
06 DINNER RECIPES 33
07 VEGETERIAN RECIPES 60
08 DESSERT RECIPES 67
09 SIDES 73
10 SNACKS 79
11 Meal Planner
12 Get in Touch

Introduction

Welcome to the world of delicious and nutritious low-carb cooking! In this cookbook, I embark on a culinary journey celebrating the art of crafting mouthwatering meals while keeping carbohydrates in check.

As an advocate of a low-carb lifestyle, I focus on whole, nutrient-dense ingredients that fuel our bodies and energise our lives. Each recipe in this cookbook is created to strike the perfect balance between flavour, texture, and nutritional value, ensuring that you savour every bite while maintaining a healthy and sustainable way of eating.

Contrary to popular belief, low-carb doesn't mean sacrificing flavour. It opens up a world of culinary possibilities as I explore inventive ways to substitute traditional high-carb ingredients with wholesome alternatives. From hearty breakfasts and vibrant salads to satisfying mains and indulgent desserts, every recipe is a testament to the idea that delicious meals can be enjoyed without compromising your commitment to a low-carb lifestyle.

Hello

Welcome to my low-carbohydrate recipe book! My name is Veronika, and I am a qualified Health coach passionate about delicious, nourishing food. I have completely changed my lifestyle two and a half years ago. I lost 30 kg and improved my digestion, asthma and indigestion to a level of being medication-free. My cookbook contains easy-to-cook recipes packed with flavour and nutrients. You will not miss your old carbohydrate life and won't need to do any calorie counting either. Enjoy your health journey with these delicious recipes!

Veronika Slavik

Health Tips

01 Use butter, coconut, or olive oil for frying and extra-virgin olive oil for drizzling over salads.

Season your meals with Himalayan pink or Celtic grey salt to boost your mineral intake. **02**

03 Meal planning is an important part of your new lifestyle.

Eat as many green vegetables as you want. **04**

05 All your carbohydrates must come from natural food.

Don't be scared to eat fat. It will fill you up for longer. **06**

07 Intermittent fasting for women should be at most 14 hours long.

Determine your low-carbohydrate daily intake yourself. What works for others might not work for you. **08**

09 Stop buying processed food and visit your local farm shop instead.

Eat mindfully and listen to your body. **10**

BREAKFAST AND BRUNCH

Mini pancakes with strawberry jam and honey-flavoured syrup

Baked egg casserole with bacon and parmesan crisps

Cinnamon granola with blueberry yoghurt

Raspberry peanut butter chia pudding

Cooked breakfast with celeriac rosti

Strawberry smoothie

Breakfast muffins

"BREAKFAST IS NOT JUST A MEAL; IT'S A DAILY OPPORTUNITY TO NOURISH YOUR BODY AND FUEL YOUR SPIRIT FOR THE CHALLENGES AHEAD." - SARAH SMITH

Mini pancakes

INGREDIENTS

- 250g almond flour
- 200 ml milk
- 3 eggs
- 30g Stevia sweetener
- butter for frying

INSTRUCTIONS

Whisk together the almond flour, milk, sweetener and eggs. Add half a teaspoon of butter to a pancake frying pan and drop a large spoonful of batter into the melted butter. Fry the pancakes on low heat as the batter needs longer to cook through than the batter with flour. Adjust the heat once you flip the pancake to medium heat. It takes 2 minutes per side to cook each pancake. Fry 3-4 pancakes at a time. Serve the mini pancakes with your favourite low-sugar jam.

6 portions

Baked egg casserole with bacon and parmesan crisps

INGREDIENTS

- 6 eggs
- 200g streaky bacon
- 150g chestnut mushrooms
- 150g Oyster mushrooms
- 300 ml double cream
- 150g Parmesan
- 20g chives
- 1 tsp Cayenne pepper
- Himalayan pink salt
- ground black pepper

INSTRUCTIONS

Preheat the oven to 200°C. Whisk the eggs with double cream, salt, ground black pepper, and Cayenne pepper. Add sliced mushrooms, diced bacon, 50g Parmesan and finely chopped chives. Mix it and pour it into a non-stick deep baking dish. Bake in the middle of the oven for 30 minutes.

Line a large shallow roasting tray with baking paper and spoon 100g parmesan in full circles all over the tray. Bake at the top of the oven for the last few minutes of baking time.

Serve the baked egg casserole with the Parmesan crisps and salad on the side.

4 portions

Cinnamon granola with blueberry yoghurt

INGREDIENTS

- 150g roasted Marcona almonds
- 150g wild blueberries
- 600g Greek yoghurt
- 50g coconut flakes
- 2 tsp ground cinammon
- walnut oil

INSTRUCTIONS

The night before, preheat the oven to 170°C. Drizzle the walnut oil over the almonds and coconut flakes in a shallow baking tray. Stir through the cinnamon and bake at the bottom of the oven for 15 minutes or until golden.

In the morning, spoon the yoghurt into a serving bowl and add the cinnamon granola and blueberries.

6 portions

Raspberry peanut butter chia pudding

INGREDIENTS

- 200 ml Greek yoghurt
- 50 ml milk
- 50g raspberries
- 30g chia seeds
- 3 tbsp peanut butter

INSTRUCTIONS

Stir all the ingredients together. Divide the mixture into two portions. Leave the pudding to thicken overnight.

2 portions

Cooked breakfast with celeriac rosti

INGREDIENTS

- 5 eggs
- 8 gluten-free sausages
- 8 rashers of bacon
- 400g chestnut mushrooms
- 1 celeriac
- 30g butter
- 50g toasted soya flour
- 3 tomatoes
- 2 garlic cloves
- 1 red chilli
- 1 tsp Cayenne pepper
- 1/3 tsp xantham gum
- olive oil
- Himalayan pink salt
- ground black pepper

INSTRUCTIONS

To make the rosti, grate the celeriac and mix it with one egg, xantham gum, soya flour, salt, and ground black pepper. Heat the frying pan, add the olive oil and fry the celeriac rosti in batches. The rostis are easily made with two tablespoons. Fry the rostis until browned on each side, flipping them halfway through. Set the rostis aside.

Simmer chopped tomatoes, Cayenne pepper, minced garlic, finely diced red chilli, and salt for the tomato sauce. The sauce takes 10-15 minutes to cook. You can use a hand blender for a smooth finish.

Meanwhile, heat the oven grill to a high setting and grill the sausages and bacon rashers.

Fry sliced mushrooms in some butter until caramelised.

Place the cracked eggs into egg poucher cups. Season them with salt and pepper. Pour 200ml water into a cooking pan, insert the poucher cups and bring the water to a boil. Lower the heat and cook the eggs for 7 minutes for runny eggs.

Serve the sausages, bacon, and mushrooms with the celeriac rosti and spicy tomato sauce. Top with the poached egg.

4 portions

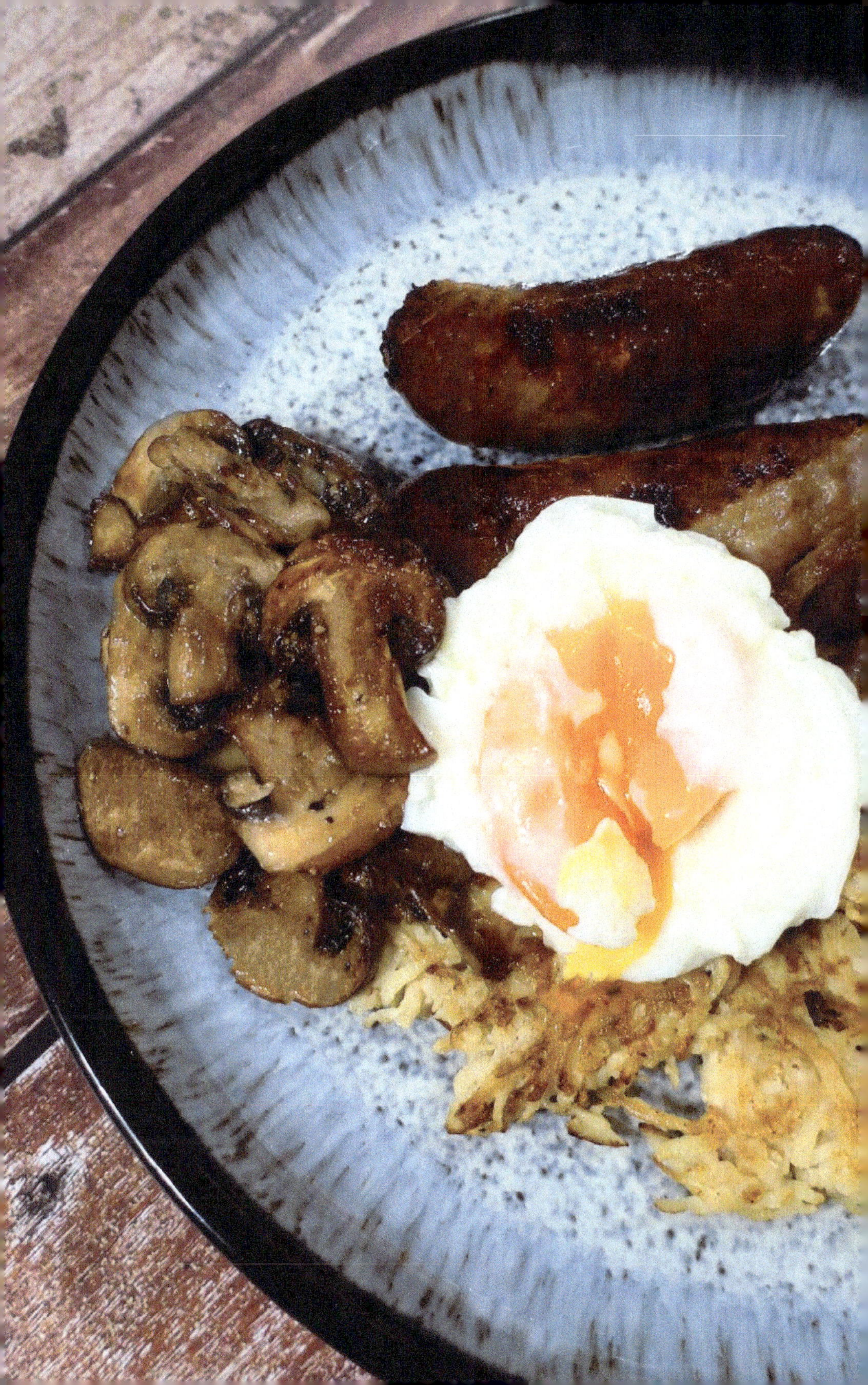

Strawberry smoothie

INGREDIENTS

- 5 strawberries
- 1 tsp cacao powder
- 1 tbsp peanut butter
- 250 ml milk

INSTRUCTIONS

Whizz all the ingredients in a blender until you end up with a smoothie.

1 portion

Breakfast muffins

INGREDIENTS

- 6 gluten-free sausages
- 250g chestnut mushrooms
- 200g baby spinach
- 100g Greek yoghurt
- 4 eggs
- 1 feta
- olive oil
- Himalayan pink salt
- ground black pepper

INSTRUCTIONS

Preheat the oven to 220°C. Pour boiled water over the spinach. Remove the sausage casings and mix the sausage meat with sliced mushrooms, eggs, yoghurt, crumbled feta and spinach. Season the mixture.

Brush some olive oil over the muffin tray. Spoon the sausage mixture into each muffin hole and bake in the middle of the oven for 25-30 minutes.

4 portions

SOUP

Mushroom soup with bacon and parmesan chip

Pumpkin soup with bacon croutons

Spicy chorizo soup

Brocolli soup with pork scratchings

"SOUP IS A FORM OF COMFORT THAT WARMS THE BODY AND SOUL. IT'S A SYMPHONY OF FLAVOURS, A HUG IN A BOWL, AND A REMINDER THAT SIMPLICITY CAN BE PROFOUNDLY SATISFYING."

Mushroom soup with bacon and parmesan chip

INGREDIENTS

- 500g chestnut mushrooms
- 250g mascarpone
- 250g streaky bacon
- 100g parmesan
- 50g butter
- 30g dried mushrooms
- 1l of chicken stock
- 1 onion
- ground black pepper
- Himalayan pink salt

INSTRUCTIONS

Pour boiled water over the dried mushrooms and leave to soak for at least 15 minutes.

Meanwhile, dice the onion and slice the mushrooms. Melt the butter in a large cooking pot and add the onion and mushrooms. Fry until softened and start to brown.

Preheat the oven to 200°C.

Add the soaked mushrooms and the soaking liquid to the cooking pot. Pour in the chicken stock and season with salt and ground black pepper. Reduce the chicken stock to 750 ml for a creamier soup.

Simmer the soup for 20 minutes.

Line a baking tray with baking paper for the parmesan chips. Shape the parmesan into 30 discs, and bake for 5 minutes or until lightly golden. Let the parmesan chips cool.

Pan-fry diced bacon on a dry pan.

Add the mascarpone to the soup and simmer for 5 minutes. Blend the soup with a hand blender. Serve the soup with parmesan chips and bacon.

4 portions

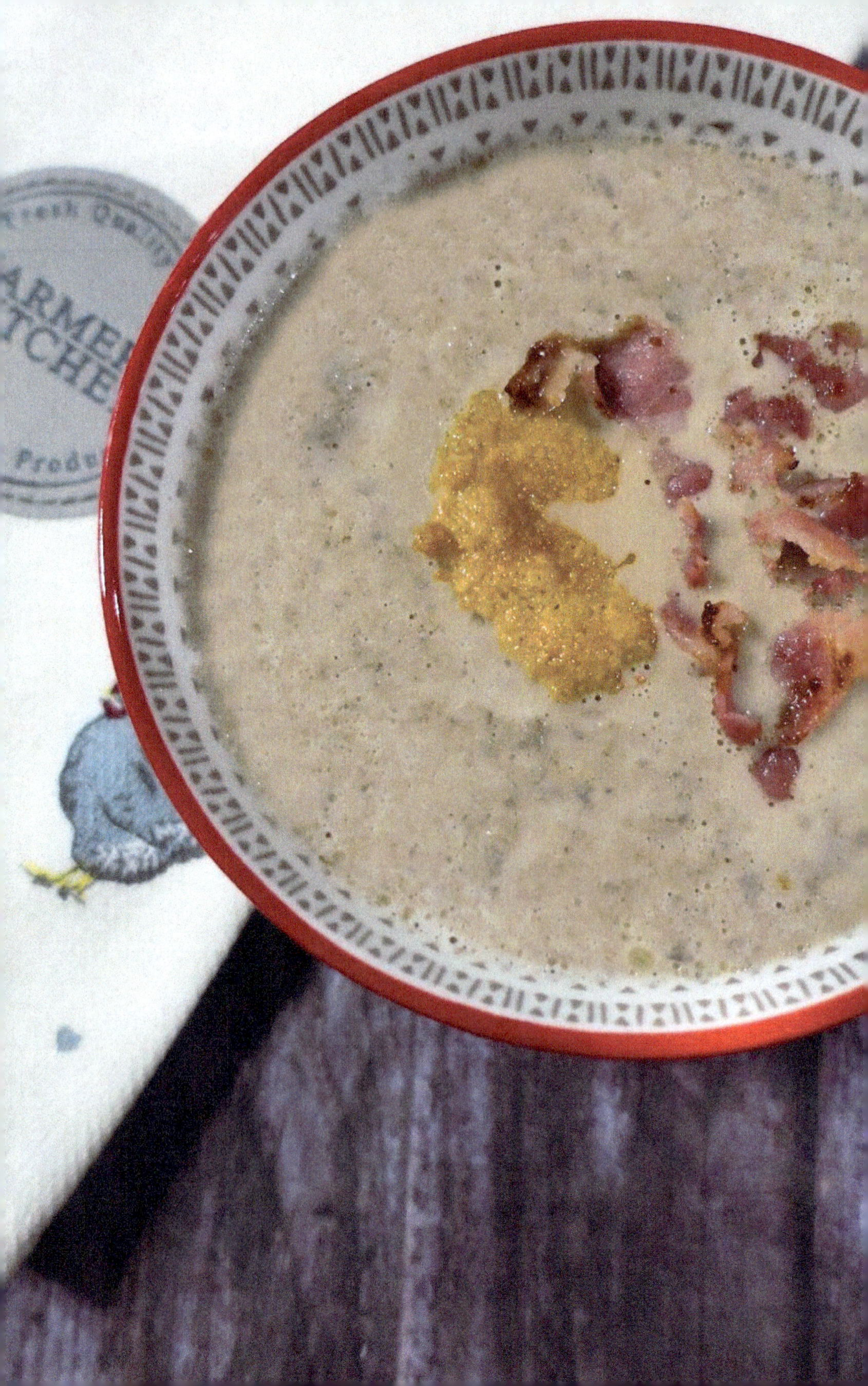

Pumpkin soup with bacon croutons

INGREDIENTS

- 1 medium size pumpkin
- 300g streaky bacon
- 4 slices of low-carb bread
- 100g mascarpone
- 50g pumpkin seeds
- 1.5l vegetable stock
- 1 tsp Himalayan pink salt
- 1 red chilli
- 1 tbsp coconut oil
- 2 garlic cloves
- 2 tsp hot smoked paprika
- ground black pepper
- olive oil

INSTRUCTIONS

Peel the pumpkin and slice it into cubes. Melt the coconut oil in a large cooking pan, add finely sliced red chilli and garlic, and stir-fry for 1-2 minutes. Add the pumpkin, vegetable stock, salt, and ground black pepper. Add less stock if you like the soup thicker. Bring the soup to a boil, turn the heat down, and cook for 30 minutes or until the pumpkin is soft.

Meanwhile, preheat the oven to 220°C. Toss the diced bacon, bread, pumpkin seeds, hot smoked paprika, and olive oil in a large roasting tray. Roast it for 10 minutes or until golden.

Stir the mascarpone into the soup. Pour the soup into a soup maker and whizz until smooth. Serve the soup with the bacon croutons.

4 portions

Spicy chorizo soup

INGREDIENTS

- 1 chorizo
- 1 onion
- 1 kohlrabi
- 1l chicken stock
- 300g sauerkraut
- 200 ml double cream
- 2 tsp Cayenne pepper
- Himalayan pink salt
- ground black pepper

INSTRUCTIONS

Fry diced chorizo and sliced onion until the onion starts to brown. Add diced kohlrabi, sauerkraut, Cayenne pepper, salt and pepper. Stir everything together. Pour in the chicken stock and bring to a boil. Turn the heat down and cook the soup for 20 minutes. Stir in the double cream, and cook it for a few minutes more.

4 portions

Brocolli soup with pork scratchings

INGREDIENTS

- 1 broccoli
- 150g stilton
- 100g pork scratchings
- a knob of a butter
- 1.5 l vegetable stock
- 1 onion
- 2 garlic cloves
- Himalayan pink salt
- ground black pepper

INSTRUCTIONS

In a large cooking pot, fry the sliced onion and minced garlic in the butter until slightly browned. Add the chopped broccoli and the vegetable stock. Bring the stock to a boiling point, turn the heat down, season the soup, and cook it for 20 minutes.

Add the stilton for the last few minutes, and blend the soup with a hand blender until smooth. Whizz the pork scratchings in a food processor.

Serve the soup with pork scratchings.

4 portions

LUNCH

Salad with goat cheese, blackberries and toasted almonds

Leftover roast meat tortilla wrap with basil cream cheese

Grilled chicken breast with kohlrabi and watermelon radish salad

Cabbage beef mince wraps

Mackerel fishcakes

Peanut butter turkey strips with rainbow chard

Roasted pumpkin, black pudding and blackberries salad

Salad with sausage meatballs, parmesan and avocado

Lettuce cup with bacon and cheese

Egg mayo

Chicken pasta salad

"ENJOY EVERY BITE, FOR IT IS NOT JUST A MEAL BUT A MOMENT OF GRATITUDE."

Salad with goat cheese, blackberries and toasted almonds

INGREDIENTS

- 150g goat cheese
- 150g blackberries
- 100g mixed salad leaves
- 50g almond flakes+ 25g for the pesto
- 50g Parmesan
- 50 ml of olive oil
- 4 tomatillos
- 1 red chilli

2 portions

INSTRUCTIONS

Whizz the tomatillos, 25g of almond flakes, red chilli, Parmesan and olive oil in a food processor. Set the pesto aside.

Toast the almond flakes in a dry frying pan until golden. This will take just a few minutes.

Toss the salad leaves with the pesto, add the sliced goat cheese and blackberries to each plate and top it with the toasted almond flakes.

Leftover roast meat tortilla wrap with basil cream cheese

INGREDIENTS

- 2 low-carb tortillas
- 100g leftover roast beef meat
- 20g fresh basil
- 50g cream cheese
- 1 small onion
- ground black pepper
- Himalayan pink salt
- Olive oil

INSTRUCTIONS

Mix chopped basil, ground black pepper, salt and cream cheese until combined.

Fry sliced onion in olive oil for 10-15 minutes on low heat. Add the roast meat and fry for a minute or two to warm it up.

Spread the basil cream cheese in the middle of each tortilla, add the onion and meat and roll the tortilla. Fry the tortilla wrap in a drizzle of olive oil from both sides.

2 portions

Grilled chicken breast with kohlrabi and watermelon radish salad

INGREDIENTS

- 2 chicken breasts skin on
- 1 kohlrabi
- 1 watermelon radish
- 100g feta
- 1/3 cabbage
- 200g sour cream
- 2 garlic cloves
- 2 tbsp milk
- 2tsp hot paprika
- ground black pepper
- Himalayan pink salt

2 portions

INSTRUCTIONS

Preheat the oven grill to the highest setting. Rub the hot paprika into both chicken breasts and grill for 5 minutes on each side or until there is no trace of pink when the meat is pierced.

Meanwhile, cut the kohlrabi into matchsticks, slice the radish and shred the cabbage.

Whisk the sour cream, salt, ground black pepper, minced garlic, and milk until the dressing is pourable.

Mix the vegetables with cubed feta and the dressing. Serve the grilled chicken breast with the salad.

Cabbage beef mince wraps

INGREDIENTS

- 6 leaves of Savoy cabbage
- 500g beef mince
- 3 garlic cloves
- 3 tsp original hot sauce
- 2 tsp soy sauce
- handful of coriander
- olive oil

INSTRUCTIONS

Cut out the hardest piece of stem. Dry fry the beef mince, coriander, and minced garlic. Add the hot sauce and soy sauce. Fry until all liquid evaporates. Spoon the beef mince into each cabbage leaf, wrap the beef in, and secure it with a cocktail stick. Drizzle with olive oil. Place the wraps into the air fryer and air fry for 7 minutes at 200°C.

2 portions

Mackerel fishcakes

INGREDIENTS

- 1 celeriac
- 300g smoked mackerel fillets
- 200g radishes
- 300g mixed leaves salad
- 100g ricotta
- 150g chilli cheese
- 1 small cucumber
- 1 large spring onion
- 1 egg
- balsamic vinegar
- ground black pepper
- Himalayan pink salt

INSTRUCTIONS

Mash the cooked, peeled celeriac, ricotta, egg, and crumbled chilli cheese to make the fish cakes. Stir in flaked mackerel, finely diced radishes, sliced spring onion, ground black pepper and salt.

Form 10 fish cakes with your hands. Place the fishcakes into the air-fryer, you might need to do this in batches, and air-fry at 200°C for 20 mins. Turn the fishcakes halfway through.

For the salad, toss the mixed leaves, diced cucumber, and a drizzle of balsamic vinegar.

Serve the fishcakes with the salad.

4 portions

Peanut butter turkey strips with rainbow chard

INGREDIENTS

- 300g turkey strips
- 200g rainbow chard
- 250g chestnut mushrooms
- 30g butter
- 2 tbsp peanut butter
- 1 red chilli
- a handful of wild garlic
- 1/2 lime
- 1 tsp Cayenne pepper
- Himalayan pink salt
- ground black pepper

INSTRUCTIONS

To make the marinade, whisk together the peanut butter, lime juice, 50 ml boiled water and the Cayenne pepper. Coat the turkey strips in the marinade and set aside.

Place the turkey strips in an air fryer in one layer and air fry them at 200°C for 20 minutes. Stir the turkey strips a couple of times to air-fry them evenly.

Meanwhile, fry the sliced mushrooms in butter until browned. Add the sliced rainbow chard, diced red chilli, sliced wild garlic, salt, and ground black pepper. Stir fry until the rainbow chard softens.

2 portions

Roasted pumpkin, black pudding and blackberries salad

INGREDIENTS

- 1/2 small pumpkin or squash
- 150g blackberries
- 4 slices of black pudding
- 1/2 lemon
- 300g mixed leaves
- 200g feta
- 1 tsp honey
- 50g mixed seeds
- 50 ml chilli olive oil
- Himalayan pink salt

2 portions

INSTRUCTIONS

Preheat the oven to 220°C. Toss the diced pumpkin with 25 ml of olive oil and salt. Roast the pumpkin in the middle of the oven for 25 minutes. Add the crumbled feta and mixed seeds for the last 5 minutes of the roasting time.

Meanwhile, fry diced black pudding in a drizzle of olive oil. Set aside.

Whisk together the lemon juice, honey and 25 ml olive oil.

Toss the blackberries, black pudding, roasted pumpkin, feta, and mixed leaves with the dressing.

Salad with sausage meatballs, parmesan and avocado

INGREDIENTS

- 200g mixed salad leaves
- 300g gluten-free sausages
- 50g parmesan
- 1 avocado
- 2 eggs
- 30g pumpkin seeds
- olive oil
- Himalayan pink salt
- ground black pepper

INSTRUCTIONS

Mix the salad leaves with sliced avocado, pumpkin seeds, 25g of parmesan, salt, ground black pepper and olive oil. Set aside.

Remove the sausages from the casings, roll the sausage meat into meatballs and fry them in a glug of olive oil until browned all over.

Meanwhile, simmer the eggs for 4 minutes. Peel the eggs' shells and cut the eggs in half. Serve the salad with sausage meatballs, egg and some extra parmesan.

2 portions

Lettuce cup with bacon and cheese

INGREDIENTS

- 200g bacon
- 150g grated Cheddar
- 1 red pepper
- 1 onion
- 50g mixed seeds
- 4 cos lettuce leaves
- olive oil
- ground black pepper
- Himalayan pink salt

4 portions

INSTRUCTIONS

Dry fry diced bacon until crispy. Add olive oil, sliced red pepper and onion, and stir fry until the vegetables soften. Season with salt and black pepper.

Fill the lettuce cups with the bacon and vegetable mixture. Sprinkle each lettuce cup with cheese and mixed seeds.

Egg mayo

INGREDIENTS

- 4 eggs
- 2 tbsp mayonnaise
- 200g soft cheese
- 6 rashers of streaky bacon
- 25g chives
- Himalayan pink salt
- ground black pepper

INSTRUCTIONS

Dry fry the diced streaky bacon until crispy.

Meanwhile, bring water to a boil in a cooking pan and cook the eggs, lowering the heat, for 4-5 minutes for a soft-boiled egg.

Peel the eggs and finely dice them. Mix the eggs with the bacon, soft cheese, and mayonnaise. Stir through the seasoning and finely chopped chives.

Serve the egg mayo with your favourite low-carb bread or low-carb crackers.

4 portions

Chicken pasta salad

INGREDIENTS

- 150g protein low-carbohydrate pasta
- 400g leftover chicken meat
- 80g rocket
- 50g pine nuts
- 1 feta
- 1 red pepper
- 1 avocado
- 3 tbsp mayonnaise
- 3 tbsp chilli sauce
- drizzle of garlic olive oil
- ground black pepper
- Himalayan pink salt

4 portions

INSTRUCTIONS

Cook the pasta as per the packaging instructions. Meanwhile, dry fry the pine nuts for a couple of minutes until golden.

Mix the cooled cooked pasta, rocket leaves, sliced red pepper, crumbled feta, diced chicken, pine nuts, sliced avocado, mayonnaise, chilli sauce, and garlic olive oil in a large bowl. Season with salt and ground black pepper.

DINNER

Pasta with meatballs and Pecorino

Meatballs with cauliflower puree and mushroom sauce

Penne with pork loin and Harissa paste

Pork chops with cheesy winter vegetables

Stuffed marrow with salmon and cream cheese

Beef hot pot with gherkins, pancetta and fried onion

Cauliflower sausage bake

"DINNER IS NOT JUST A MEAL; IT'S A CELEBRATION OF FLAVOURS AND TOGETHERNESS."

Meatloaf with kohlrabi wedges

Cheesy spicy pork loins

Pork chops with cheese biscuits crumble and purple sprouting broccoli

Pork fillet in herb butter with celeriac fries

Lamb and cauliflower moussaka

Cauliflower rice with chorizo, mushrooms and chives

Pork patties with Brie and dry mushrooms

Fish and chips

Chicken stuffed with spicy tomato chorizo mascarpone

Cauliflower chorizo creamy bake

Naked turkey burger with coconut tenderstem broccoli

Venison strips with squash puree

Pork loin skewer

Stir-fry pork bun with celeriac crisp

Roasted duck crown with swede mash and red wine dark chocolate sauce

Pork meatballs stir-fry

Pasta with meatballs and Pecorino

INGREDIENTS

- 400g Edamame fettuccine
- 400g Beef mince
- 100g tomato sauce (no added sugar)
- 100 ml vegetable stock
- 50g Pecorino cheese
- 1 small onion
- 1 leek
- 2 celery sticks
- 3 tsp Harissa seasoning
- ground black pepper
- Himalayan pink salt
- olive oil

4 portions

INSTRUCTIONS

Season the beef mince with Harissa seasoning and some ground black pepper. Roll the seasoned beef mince into 20 meatballs.

Slice the onion, leek and celery sticks. Fry the vegetables in some olive oil for 5 minutes. Add the vegetable stock and tomato sauce. Simmer until the sauce thickens.

Cook the pasta in salted water as per the manufacturer's instructions.

Air-fry the meatballs at 200°C for 15 minutes.

Stir the vegetables through the fettuccine, add the meatballs and grate the Pecorino over the pasta.

Meatballs with cauliflower puree and mushroom sauce

INGREDIENTS

- 1 cauliflower
- 500g beef mince
- 250g chestnut mushrooms
- 450 ml double cream
- 50g butter
- 30g almond flour
- ground black pepper
- Himalayan pink salt

INSTRUCTIONS

Season the beef mince with ground black pepper and salt. Shape the meat into balls, place them in an air fryer, and fry at 200°C for 12 minutes, 6 minutes on each side.

Meanwhile, roughly chop the cauliflower. Place it into a cooking pan. Salt the water and bring it to the boiling point. Once the water reaches boiling, turn the heat down and simmer the cauliflower for 20 minutes. Strain the water from the cooking pot. Add 150 ml of the double cream and the butter. Blend the cauliflower in a blender.

Slice the mushrooms. Fry the mushrooms in 30g of butter until browned. Stir in the almond flour, pour over the rest of the double cream, season with ground black pepper, and simmer for 1-2 minutes.

Serve the meatballs with the cauliflower puree and mushroom sauce.

Tips:

The meatballs can be roasted in the oven. Preheat the oven to 200°C. Roast the meatballs for 10 minutes or until browned.

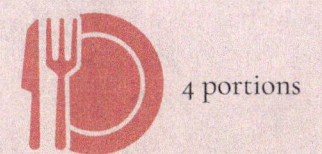

4 portions

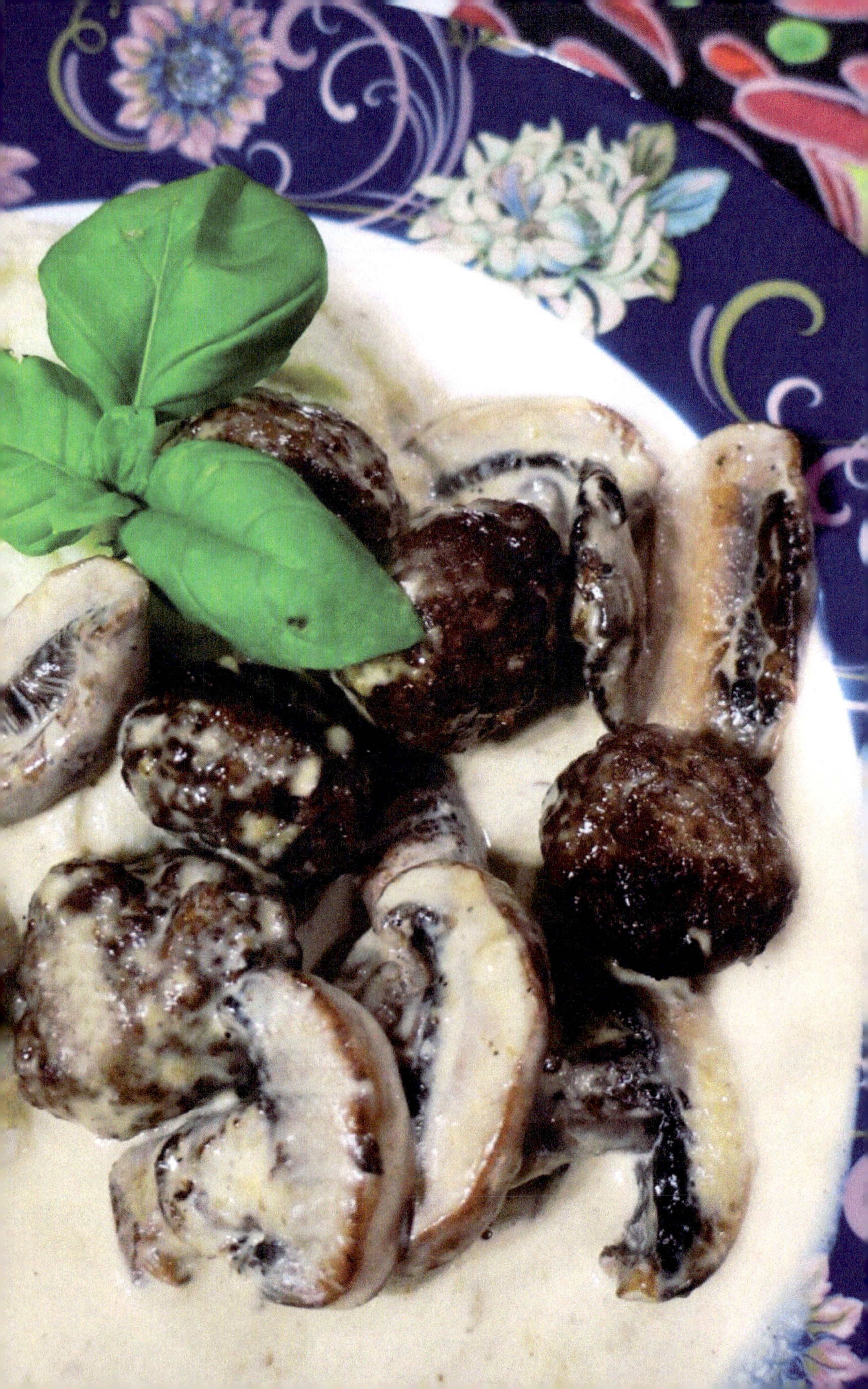

Penne with pork loin and Harissa paste

INGREDIENTS

- 400g Low-carb penne pasta
- 150g rainbow chard
- 100 ml thick double cream
- 4 pork loins
- 1 leek
- 6 tsp Harissa paste
- 2 tbsp chilli olive oil
- olive oil
- ground black pepper
- Himalayan pink salt

INSTRUCTIONS

Preheat the oven to its highest setting. Mix chilli olive oil with 2 tsp of Harissa paste and brush it over the pork loins. Grill the pork loins under an oven grill for 5-6 mins.

Meanwhile, cook the pasta in salted simmering water per the packaging instructions.

Fry the sliced leek and rainbow chard in some olive oil until softened. Add the rest of the Harrisa paste, ground black pepper, double cream and a splash of pasta cooking water. Simmer the sauce for a minute. Stir the pasta through the sauce and serve it with the pork loin.

4 portions

Pork chops with cheesy winter vegetables

INGREDIENTS

- 2 pork chops
- 4-6 rashers of streaky bacon
- 1 carrot matchsticks
- 1/2 sliced celeriac
- 1/2 sliced swede
- 1 egg
- 100g Cheddar
- 150 ml double cream
- 1 tsp hot paprika + extra for the pork chops
- 1 tsp ground black pepper
- 1tsp celery salt
- 30g butter
- olive oil

INSTRUCTIONS

Preheat the oven to 200ºC. Toss all the vegetables with ground black pepper, celery salt, and hot paprika in two small roasting dishes. Whisk together the egg, double cream, and grated cheddar. Pour this mixture over the vegetables, slice the butter, and dot it over the top. Roast the vegetables for 45 minutes or until soft in the middle.

Meanwhile, mix some olive oil with hot paprika. Brush it over the pork chops from both sides, wrap two streaky bacon rashers around each pork chop and grill for 6 minutes on each side. Serve the pork chops with cheesy vegetables.

2 portions

Stuffed marrow with salmon and cream cheese

INGREDIENTS

- 1 big marrow
- 160g hot smoked salmon
- 150g cream cheese
- 250g mozzarella
- 50g pine nuts
- 20g basil
- 5 tsp garlic paste
- 1/2 lemon
- ground black pepper
- Himalayan pink salt

INSTRUCTIONS

Preheat the oven to 210°C. Half the marrow lengthways and scoop up the flesh from both halves. Salt the marrow and pre-bake for 20 mins. Meanwhile, mix flaked salmon, cream cheese, garlic paste, basil, half a lemon juice, and some ground black pepper.

Pat dry the marrow halves. Spoon the filling into both halves. Add mozzarella slices and pine nuts on top. Place under the grill for 2-5 minutes or until golden.

2 portions

Beef hot pot with gherkins, pancetta and fried onion

INGREDIENTS

- 400g diced beef for stewing
- 200g gherkins
- 80g pancetta
- 2 onions
- 1 carrot
- 1/2 celeriac
- 1 tbsp hot sauce or tomato paste
- 2 tsp smoked paprika
- a knob of butter
- olive oil
- ground black pepper
- Himalayan pink salt

4 portions

INSTRUCTIONS

Fry one diced onion and beef in a knob of butter until browned. Add the hot sauce, chopped carrot and celeriac, smoked paprika, salt and ground black pepper and 1 litre of boiled water. Cook over slow heat for 4 hours.

Meanwhile, slowly fry the pancetta and sliced onion in a glug of olive oil for 15 minutes.

Serve the beef hot pot with gherkins, fried pancetta, onion and your favourite side.

Cauliflower sausage bake

INGREDIENTS

- 1 cauliflower
- 300g gluten-free sausages
- 100g rainbow chard
- 200g chestnut mushrooms
- 150g grated mozzarella
- 200 ml of double cream
- 200 ml milk
- 75g butter
- 30g coconut flour
- 2 tsp mustard
- ground black pepper
- Himalayan pink salt

INSTRUCTIONS

Preheat the oven to 200°C. Place the cauliflower florets, sliced mushrooms, sliced chard, and diced sausages into a deep roasting dish. Season with salt and ground black pepper.

Melt the butter in a medium-sized cooking pot. Add the flour and mustard, stir until thick and pour over the milk and double cream. Continue whisking the sauce until it starts to boil.

Pour the sauce over the cauliflower and sausages. Spread the grated mozzarella cheese over the top. Bake for 40-45 minutes. Cover the bake with foil if the top starts to brown fast.

4 portions

Chicken stuffed with spicy tomato chorizo mascarpone

INGREDIENTS

- 2 chicken breasts
- 100g chorizo
- 100g mascarpone
- 50g cherry tomatoes
- ground black pepper
- Himalayan pink salt

INSTRUCTIONS

Preheat the oven to 220°C. Fry diced chorizo in a large frying pan. Add the tomatoes and simmer until softened. Mix the mascarpone with the chorizo and tomatoes. Season the chicken breasts with salt and ground black pepper. Insert a knife at the top of each chicken breast to create a pocket. Push the blade in, but don't cut through.

Stuff the chicken with the mascarpone stuffing and brush the leftover mascarpone over the chicken breasts.

Roast the chicken breasts in the middle of the oven for 25 minutes.

2 portions

Cauliflower chorizo creamy bake

INGREDIENTS

- 1 small cauliflower (purple when in season)
- 220g chorizo
- 200ml red wine
- 150g Philadelphia cheese
- 100g green olives
- 30g dry mushrooms
- 1 onion
- ground black pepper
- Himalayan pink salt

INSTRUCTIONS

Soak the dry mushrooms in 250 ml of boiled water for 15 minutes.
Preheat the oven to 220°C. Add the cauliflower florets to salted water and bring to a boil. Cook slowly for 10 minutes. Set aside.

Fry the sliced onion and chorizo in their juices for a few minutes. Pour in the red wine and the mushrooms with the liquid. Add the halved olives and Philadelphia cheese, stir until the cheese blends in, and add the cooked cauliflower florets. Season them with ground black pepper and salt. Transfer the cooking pan contents into individual ramekins and bake in the middle of the oven for 20 minutes.

2 portions

Naked turkey burger with coconut tenderstem broccoli

INGREDIENTS

- 400g turkey mince
- 400g tenderstem broccoli
- 200 ml coconut milk
- 30g coconut flakes
- 1 tbsp coconut oil
- 1tsp chilli flakes
- 3 tsp ginger paste
- 1 tbsp peanut butter
- a handful of coriander
- 1 red chilli
- 2 garlic cloves
- 1 tsp hot paprika
- Himalayan pink salt

4 portions

INSTRUCTIONS

Mix the turkey mince, peanut butter, diced red chilli, minced garlic, hot paprika and salt. Shape the mixture into four burgers. Place the burgers into an air fryer and air-fry them at 200°C for 18 minutes, 9 minutes on each side.

Meanwhile, fry the tenderstem broccoli in the coconut oil for a few minutes. Add the ginger paste, chilli flakes, and coriander. Pour over the coconut milk and simmer until the coconut milk evaporates and the broccoli softens. Top the broccoli with coconut flakes.

Venison strips with squash puree

INGREDIENTS

- 500g venison strips
- 500 ml of beef stock
- 150g Oyster mushrooms
- 150g Shiitake mushrooms
- 150 ml milk
- 20g butter
- 1 squash
- 1 small onion
- 2 spoons of beef dripping
- 2 tsp Turmeric
- 1tsp dried marjoram
- ground black pepper
- Himalayan pink salt

INSTRUCTIONS

Preheat the oven to 220°C. Cut the squash into quarters, remove the seeds, and roast in the middle of the oven for 40-50 minutes.

Stir-fry the venison strips in 1 tbsp of beef dripping until browned. Remove with a slotted spoon and set aside.

Add sliced onion and mushrooms into the pan, and add more beef dripping if needed. Add black pepper, salt, marjoram, and stir-fry for five minutes, and then pour the beef stock over. Simmer for 10-15 minutes. Return the venison strips to the pan and keep it warm.

Scoop the squash from its peel and blend it with turmeric, milk and butter until the puree is lump-free. Serve the venison strips with the squash puree.

4 portions

Pork loin skewer

INGREDIENTS

- 400g pork filet
- 200g bacon
- 1 small white onion
- 1 red pepper
- 1tsp hot paprika
- 1tsp dried coriander
- 2tsp ground black pepper
- 2tsp garlic
- 1tsp chilli flakes
- 1tsp mustard powder
- olive oil

INSTRUCTIONS

Slice the pork filet thinly and cut the bacon into three pieces. Marinate the meat in the olive oil and the spices.

Skewer the pork fillet, bacon, sliced onion and red pepper onto a metal skewer.

Grill for 10-15 minutes or until browned all over.

4 portions

Stir-fry pork bun with celeriac crisp

INGREDIENTS

- 500g pork stir-fry strips
- 250 ml of olive oil
- 200ml Greek yoghurt
- 20g chives
- 2 garlic cloves
- 4 low-carbohydrate buns
- 1 red pepper
- 1 onion
- 1/2 celeriac
- Himalayan pink salt
- ground black pepper

INSTRUCTIONS

Heat the olive oil in a small cooking pan. Slice the peeled celeriac on a mandoline, and deep-fry the slices in batches for 60-90 seconds. Season with some salt and set aside.

Pour some of the used olive oil into a frying pan. Add the pork strips, sliced pepper and onion, season with ground black pepper and some salt, and stir fry until golden.

Stir minced garlic and finely chopped chives through the yoghurt.

Spoon the garlic yoghurt into a sliced bun, add the pork and serve the pork bun with the celeriac crisps and some salad on the side.

4 portions

Roasted duck crown with swede mash and red wine dark chocolate sauce

---

INGREDIENTS

- 1.2kd duck crown
- 1 large swede
- 150 ml red wine
- 50g dark chocolate
- 2 tsp Cayenne pepper
- 50 ml milk
- 50g butter
- Himalayan pink salt
- ground black pepper

INSTRUCTIONS

Preheat the oven to 220°C. Roast the duck crown in the middle of the oven for 1 hour and 30 minutes, basting it frequently with the released duck fat.

Simmer the diced and peeled swede in salted water for 15-20 minutes.

Blend the cooked swede, milk, Cayenne pepper, and butter until smooth.

Meanwhile, simmer the red wine and dark chocolate until the sauce thickens.

Serve the sliced duck meat with the swede mash and the red wine dark chocolate sauce.

2 portions

Pork meatballs stir-fry

INGREDIENTS

- 500g pork mince
- 400g konjac noodles
- 1 carrot
- 2 spring onions
- 2 pak choi
- 1 red chilli
- 2 garlic cloves
- 4 tbsp soy sauce
- garlic olive oil
- ground black pepper
- Himalayan pink salt

INSTRUCTIONS

Mix the pork mince, salt and ground black pepper and shape it into the meatballs. Air fry in the air fryer at 200°C for 15 mins. Alternatively, roast in the oven preheated to 220°C until golden.

Meanwhile, stir-fry the sliced pak choi in a glug of garlic olive oil for a few minutes. Add carrot ribbons, sliced spring onions, finely chopped red chilli, and garlic and stir fry for another minute or two. Stir in the soy sauce, and fry for a few more minutes. Add the konjac noodles, stir until all is combined, and serve with the pork meatballs.

4 portions

Meatloaf with kohlrabi wedges

INGREDIENTS

- olive oil
- 1 small onion
- 2 slices of low-carb bread
- 1 pack of feta
- 1 large spring onion
- 500g minced beef 15% fat
- 1 tsp chilli flakes
- 4 tsp Ras el Hanout spice
- 2 eggs
- 2 large kohlrabi
- 2tsp garlic powder
- ground black pepper
- Himalayan pink salt

4 portions

INSTRUCTIONS

Preheat the oven to 220°C. Fry the finely diced onion in a glug of olive oil until golden. Whizz the bread slices in a food processor. Mix the breadcrumbs, fried shallots, crumbled feta, minced beef, ground black pepper, salt, chopped spring onion, Ras el Hanout, and two eggs in a large mixing bowl. Shape the mixture into two loaves and place them in a deep roasting dish. Bake the meatloaves in the centre of the oven for 30 minutes.

Peel and slice the kohlrabi into wedges. Mix them with a good splash of olive oil, chilli flakes, and garlic powder. Air fry in an air fryer at 200°C for 20 minutes.

Serve the sliced meatloaf with the kohlrabi wedges.

Cheesy spicy pork loins

INGREDIENTS

- 2 pork loins
- 150g grated Cheddar
- 150g spinach
- 80g smoked pancetta
- a jar of jalapenos
- 1 leek
- 1 white onion
- 2 tbsp cajun rub
- olive oil
- ground black pepper
- Himalayan pink salt

INSTRUCTIONS

Preheat the oven grill to 240°C. In a food processor, whizz the grated Cheddar and jalapenos until combined. Rub the Cajun seasoning into the pork loins. Grill the pork loins for around 3 minutes on one side, then turn them over and cook on the other for 1-2 minutes. Top the pork loins with the cheese and jalapenos and grill until the cheese melts.

Meanwhile, fry the diced smoked pancetta and sliced onion until the onion starts to brown. Add some olive oil, spinach, sliced leek, ground black pepper and salt, and fry the vegetables until the spinach is wilted and the leek is soft. Serve the vegetables with cheesy pork loins.

2 portions

Pork chops with cheese biscuits crumble and purple sprouting broccoli

INGREDIENTS

- 4 pork chops
- 4 large cheese biscuits
- 400g purple sprouting broccoli
- 100g mascarpone
- 2 tsp Harissa paste
- 3 tsp garlic powder
- 2tsp Chipotle Cayenne pepper
- olive oil

INSTRUCTIONS

Preheat the oven to 220°C. Whizz the cheese biscuits in a food processor and set them aside. Whisk the Harissa paste with the mascarpone. Spread the mascarpone over each pork chop and add the biscuit crumb on top of it.

Roast the pork chops for 15 minutes. Meanwhile, toss the purple-sprouting broccoli with olive oil, Chipotle Cayenne pepper and garlic powder. Stir-fry the purple sprouting broccoli for 2-3 minutes, cover the pan with a lid and continue cooking until it softens.

Find the recipe for cheese biscuits in the snack section of the cookbook.

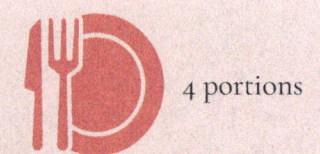

4 portions

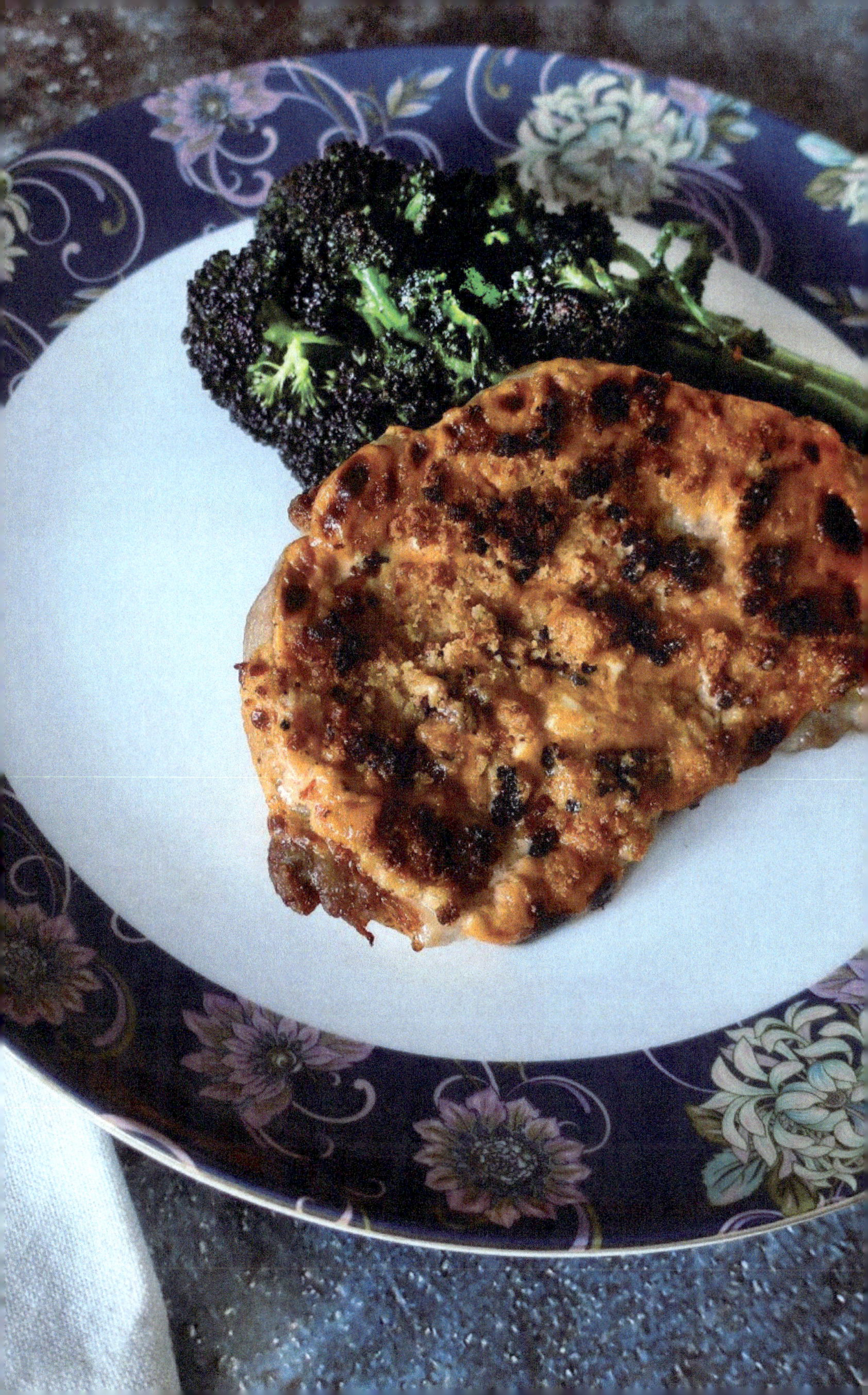

Pork fillet in herb butter with celeriac fries

INGREDIENTS

- 500g pork fillet
- 50g butter
- 50g basil
- 50g cream cheese
- 50g Parmesan
- 20g coriander
- 1 celeriac
- 4 tsp chipotle chilli powder
- 4 tsp mustard powder
- 6 tsp olive oil
- ground black pepper
- Himalayan pink salt

2 portions

INSTRUCTIONS

Preheat the oven to 220°C. Season the meat with salt and ground black pepper. Pour olive oil into a large frying pan, and sear the pork fillet from all sides. Set aside.

Whizz the basil, coriander, 2 tsp chipotle chilli powder, 2 tsp mustard powder, and butter in a food processor.

Place the pork fillet in an oven dish, and brush the herby butter onto the top and the sides of the fillet. Roast the meat for 13-15 mins.

Stir the celeriac matchsticks with 3 tsp olive oil, chipotle chilli, mustard powder, and salt.

Air-fry the celeriac fries in an air-fryer at 200°C for 20 minutes. Toss several times during the frying time.

Mix the cream cheese, Parmesan, 1 tsp of ground black pepper, and olive oil for the Parmesan dip.

Lamb and cauliflower moussaka

INGREDIENTS

- 400g lamb mince
- 350g no added sugar tomato sauce
- 400g beef stock
- 150 ml milk
- 1 cauliflower
- 2 aubergines
- 2 garlic cloves
- 1 onion
- 50g butter
- 3tsp Cayenne pepper
- ground black pepper
- Himalayan pink salt

INSTRUCTIONS

Fry the lamb mince in a dry pan until browned. Add diced aubergines and fry for another 5 minutes. Season the meat and aubergines with salt, ground black pepper and Cayenne pepper. Pour in the tomato sauce and the beef stock, and simmer with a lid on for 15 minutes.

Meanwhile, cook the cauliflower florets in salted water until soft, about 20 minutes. Place the cooked cauliflower florets, butter, and milk in a blender and blend them into a puree.

Preheat the oven to 220°C. Spoon the meat and aubergines into a deep roasting dish. Spread the cauliflower puree over the top. Bake it in the middle of the oven for 25 minutes or until golden.

4 portions

Cauliflower rice with chorizo, mushrooms and chives

INGREDIENTS

- 1 cauliflower
- 1 chorizo
- 400g chestnut mushrooms
- 150ml rose or white wine
- 30g Parmesan
- 500 ml chicken stock
- 100g green beans
- a handful of chives
- 2 tsp Cayenne pepper
- ground black pepper
- Himalayan pink salt

INSTRUCTIONS

Whizz the cauliflower florets in a food processor to create cauliflower rice.

Heat a large frying pan, add diced chorizo, and fry until it releases its juices. Remove with a slotted spoon and set it aside. Leave the chorizo juices in the frying pan, add sliced mushrooms and brown them all over. Add the cauliflower rice and the wine. Simmer until it evaporates. Return the chorizo to the pan, add the green beans, and season with Cayenne pepper, salt, and ground black pepper. Pour the chicken stock in and cook on low heat until the liquid evaporates. Stir in the Parmesan and sprinkle with finely chopped chives.

4 portions

Pork patties with Brie and dry mushrooms

INGREDIENTS

- 400g pork mince
- 100g Brie
- 30g dried mushrooms
- 1tsp chipotle chilli
- 100g rocket salad
- 100g mixed leaves
- 1 diced avocado
- 1/2 sliced cucumber
- 2 soft-boiled eggs
- 30g roasted pumpkin seeds
- 3 sliced spring onions
- ground black pepper
- Himalayan pink salt
- olive oil

INSTRUCTIONS

Pour boiled water over the dried porcini and let it stand for 10-15 minutes. Mix the finely chopped porcini, 2 tbsp of porcini liquid, pork mince, chipotle chilli and salt.

To make the patties, add a slice of Brie to every two spoonfuls of pork mince into the middle of the meat and enclose the pork mince around the Brie. Air-fry at 200°C for 18-20 minutes.

Mix all the salad ingredients and serve the pork patties with the salad.

2 portions

Fish and chips

INGREDIENTS

- 2 cod fillets
- 2 kohlrabi
- 2 tsp coconut oil
- 50g almond flour
- handful of wild garlic
- 2 tsp chilli flakes
- Himalayan pink salt
- ground black pepper

2 portions

INSTRUCTIONS

Preheat the oven to 220°C. Season the almond flour with salt, ground black pepper, finely chopped wild garlic, and chilli flakes. Cut each cod fillet into two pieces and coat them in the seasoned almond flour.

Peel and slice the kohlrabi into wedges and mix them with salt and ground black pepper. Dollop the coconut oil on top of the chips and roast them for 15-20 minutes. Stir the chips in the oil several times during roasting. Add any leftover spiced almond flour to the chips for the last 5 minutes, stirring it in.

Add the cod to the turnip chips for the last 10 minutes of roasting, turning the fish halfway through.

VEGETARIAN

Pumpkin vegetable bake

Vegetable patties with turnip chips

Paneer spicy cauli rice

Harissa tofu with broccoli puree and kale crisps

Roasted peppers and tofu bake

"EATING VEGETABLES IS A DELICIOUS WAY TO NOURISH YOUR BODY AND CELEBRATE THE VIBRANT COLOURS OF NATURE."

Pumpkin vegetable bake

INGREDIENTS

- 1 medium size pumpkin
- 1 small celery
- 200g Cavolo Nero
- 165g cream cheese
- 200g mozzarella
- 300 ml vegetable stock
- 50g pumpkin seeds
- 2 tsp Cayenne pepper
- Himalayan pink salt

INSTRUCTIONS

Preheat the oven to 200°C. Cut the pumpkin into wedges, discard the seeds, and roast it for 10-15 minutes or until it softens and is easy to peel.

Meanwhile, whisk the cream cheese and vegetable stock in a pot over medium heat, season with Cayenne pepper and salt, and set aside.

Peel the pumpkin. In a deep-roasting dish, add peeled, sliced celery to the bottom of the dish, a layer of Cavolo Nero, and sliced pumpkin, finishing with mozzarella.

Bake the layered vegetables for 35 minutes. Add the pumpkin seeds and return the dish to the oven for another 3-5 minutes.

4 portions

Vegetable patties with turnip chips

INGREDIENTS

- 300g radishes
- 250g chestnut mushrooms
- 1 pack halloumi
- 2 shallots
- 100g cashew nuts
- 700g turnips
- 200g purple sprouting broccoli
- 2 low-carb bread slices
- 1 egg
- olive oil
- butter
- ground black pepper
- cayenne pepper
- Himalayan pink salt

INSTRUCTIONS

Place the radishes into a food processor and chop them into small pieces. Set it aside. Chop the mushrooms and shallots in the food processor, and fry them in a knob of butter until brown. Place the mushrooms and shallots in the mixing bowl.

Preheat the oven to 220°C. Peel and cut the turnips into large chunks and coat them with olive oil and cayenne pepper. Add the purple sprouting broccoli into the tray with turnip chips. Bake the turnip chips at the top of the oven for 20 minutes or until soft in the middle and golden.

Squeeze the excess water from the radishes and add them to the mixing bowl. Toast the bread slices in the toaster and whizz them in the food processor. Add the egg, grated halloumi, chopped cashew nuts, breadcrumbs, ground black pepper, salt and cayenne pepper to the mixing bowl. Mix all the ingredients and shape the mixture into the patties. Place the patties in a shallow roasting tray, drizzle olive oil over them, and roast them for 15 minutes. Serve the patties with the turnip chips.

4 portions

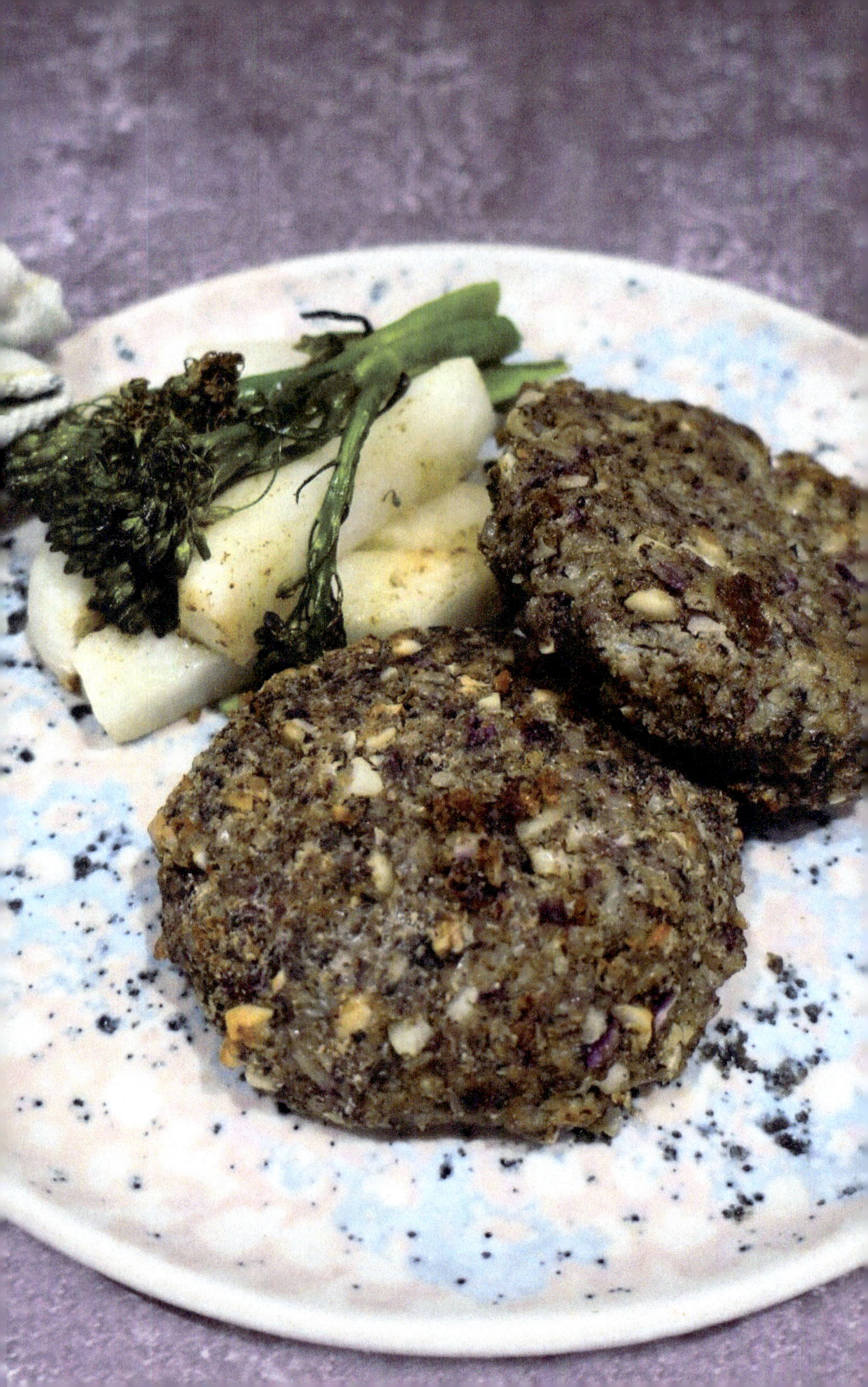

Paneer spicy cauli rice

INGREDIENTS

- 2 Paneer cheese
- 1 cauliflower
- 400 ml coconut milk
- 100g spinach
- 100g baby tomatoes
- 4 tsp Harissa spice
- 1 onion
- 1 red chilli
- olive oil
- Himalayan pink salt

INSTRUCTIONS

Fry finely diced onion, red chilly and the Harissa spice in olive oil. Add paneer cut into cubes, tomatoes, salt, and spinach. Simmer for a few minutes until the spinach is wilted.

Meanwhile, cut the cauliflower into florets and whiz the florets in a food processor to create a rice texture. Add the cauliflower rice and coconut milk to the pan and cook uncovered until the cauliflower rice thickens 10-15 minutes.

4 portions

Harissa tofu with broccoli puree and kale crisps

INGREDIENTS

- 1 large broccoli
- 500g tofu
- 300g chestnut mushrooms
- 100g curly kale
- 1/2 tsp Himalayan pink salt
- 1 tbsp coconut oil
- 2 tbsp Harissa paste
- 50g butter
- 100ml milk
- olive oil
- 1 tsp Cayenne pepper
- ground black pepper

INSTRUCTIONS

Simmer the broccoli florets in salted water for 15-20 minutes.

Meanwhile, slice the mushrooms and fry them in 25g of butter until golden. Season with ground black pepper and set aside.

Preheat the oven to 150°C. Torn the kale into bite-size pieces and toss it with olive oil, Cayenne pepper and some ground black pepper. Roast slowly for 25 minutes.

Cut the tofu into cubes, toss it with Harissa paste, and fry in the coconut oil for 10 minutes until golden. Add the mushrooms and set aside.

Blend the cooked broccoli, milk, and leftover butter until smooth.

Serve the puree with the tofu and crispy kale.

4 portions

Roasted peppers and tofu bake

INGREDIENTS

- 400g smoked tofu
- 2 red peppers
- 200g spinach
- 2 packs of konjac rice
- garlic olive oil
- ground black pepper
- Himalayan pink salt

INSTRUCTIONS

Preheat the oven to 220°C. Boil water in a kettle and pour it over the spinach. Stir the spinach and cubed tofu through the konjac rice. Season the rice and spread sliced red peppers over the rice and tofu mixture.

Bake the rice in the middle of the oven for 20 minutes.

4 portions

DESSERT

Blackberry chocolate chia pudding

Strawberry fool

Chocolate granola and berry traybake

Blueberry ice-cream

Peanut butter cheesecake

"DESSERTS ARE THE FAIRY TALES OF THE KITCHEN, A HAPPILY-EVER-AFTER TO SUPPER." - TERRI GUILLEMETS.

Blackberry chocolate chia pudding

INGREDIENTS

- 6 tbsp chia seeds
- 50g dark chocolate
- 375 ml almond milk
- 2 tbsp Stevia liquid sweetener
- 100g blackberries

INSTRUCTIONS

Melt the chocolate in a heatproof bowl set over a cooking pan with simmering water. Pour the almond milk over the chia seeds, add the sweetener and stir in the hot melted chocolate.

Refrigerate the pudding overnight. Serve the pudding with the blackberries.

4 portions

Strawberry fool

INGREDIENTS

- 300g strawberries
- 300 ml of whipping cream
- 100g almond flour
- 50g butter
- 25g almond flakes
- 2 tsp Stevia liquid sweetener

INSTRUCTIONS

Preheat the oven to 200°C. Rub the butter into the almond flour mixed with the sweetener. Spread it over a shallow baking tray and bake it for 5-10 minutes. Add the almond flakes for the last few minutes.

Slice the strawberries. Whip the whipping cream into the soft peaks.

Layer the strawberry slices, the whipped cream, and the crumble. Decorate the dessert with more strawberry slices.

4 portions

Chocolate and berry traybake

INGREDIENTS

- 200g butter
- 50g Stevia sweetener
- 100g blueberries
- 100g raspberries
- 250g almond flour
- 80g dark chocolate buutons
- 100g Greek yoghurt

10 portions

INSTRUCTIONS

Preheat the oven to 180°C. Cream the butter and the sweetener with a hand mixer. Add the yoghurt, eggs and flour and mix until combined. Stir in the berries and dark chocolate buttons. Bake for 25-30 minutes. Let it cool in the tray before cutting it into portions.

Blueberry ice-cream

INGREDIENTS

- 200g frozen blueberries
- 15 ml Stevia liquid
- 200 ml double cream
- 150g Philadelphia cheese
- 50g almond flakes

4 portions

INSTRUCTIONS

Blend all the ingredients in a blender. Freeze the ice cream for 4-6 hours. Remove it from the fridge 2 hours before serving.

Toast the almond flakes in a dry frying pan until slightly browned.

Serve the ice cream with the toasted almonds.

Peanut butter cheesecake

INGREDIENTS

- 500g cream cheese
- 300ml double cream
- 100g peanut butter
- 3 tsp Stevia liquid
- 4 gelatine leaves
- 150g almond flour
- 100g butter

INSTRUCTIONS

Soak the gelatine leaves in cold water for 5 minutes. Transfer the gelatine with 100 ml water to a cooking pan and heat it slowly. Don't bring the water to a boil. Once the gelatine dissolves, take the pan off the heat.

Stir the cooled gelatine with the cream cheese, double cream, stevia liquid and peanut butter.

Whizz the butter and the almond flour in a food processor until having a breadcrumb texture.

Line a cake tin with baking paper and press the almond mixture into the base. Pour the cheesecake mixture over the almond base and refrigerate for at least 4 hours.

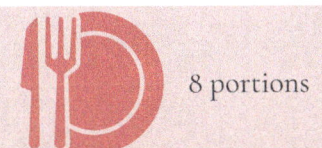

8 portions

SIDES

Tenderstem broccoli with garlic breadcrumbs

Roasted Brussels sprouts

Spicy cauliflower rice

Garlic cauliflower puree

Creamy green vegetables

"SIDE DISHES ARE THE UNSUNG HEROES OF THE MEAL, QUIETLY COMPLEMENTING THE MAIN COURSE WITH THEIR FLAVORFUL PRESENCE."

Tenderstem broccoli with garlic breadcrumbs

INGREDIENTS

- 200g tenderstem broccoli
- 2 slices of low-carb bread
- 2 garlic cloves
- 1 tsp Cayenne pepper
- chilli olive oil

INSTRUCTIONS

Place the tenderstem broccoli into a large frying pan, add a splash of water and steam for 5 minutes.

Whizz the bread, garlic and Cayenne pepper in a food processor.

Stir the breadcrumbs through the tenderstem broccoli, drizzle some chilli olive oil over and fry for another 2 minutes.

2 portions

Roasted Brussels sprouts

INGREDIENTS

- 500g Brussels sprouts
- 200g diced bacon
- 100g grated Cheddar cheese
- 25g Pumpkin seeds
- 1/2 tsp Himalayan pink salt
- ground black pepper
- olive oil

INSTRUCTIONS

Preheat the oven to 220°C. Cook the Brussels sprouts in a salted simmering water for 10-15 minutes. Fry the diced bacon in some olive oil. Set aside. Stir the bacon, pumpkin seeds, and ground black pepper through the Brussels sprouts. Spread the grated cheese over the dish and roast it for 10 minutes.

4 portions

Spicy cauliflower rice

INGREDIENTS

- 1 cauliflower
- 25g chives
- 2 garlic cloves
- 1 onion
- 2 tsp hot smoked paprika
- Himalayan pink salt
- ground black pepper
- olive oil

INSTRUCTIONS

Fry the sliced onion and minced garlic in a glug of olive oil until lightly browned.

Cut the cauliflower into florets and whizz them into a food processor. Add the cauliflower rice to the pan and season with salt, ground black pepper and hot smoked paprika. Stir-fry the rice for 2-3 minutes. Finely chop the chives and stir them through the rice before serving.

2 portions

Garlic cauliflower puree

INGREDIENTS

- 1 cauliflower
- 50g Parmesan
- 50ml garlic cold-pressed organic rapeseed oil
- 100g Greek yoghurt
- Himalayan pink salt

INSTRUCTIONS

Slowly cook the cauliflower florets in salted boiling water for 15-20 minutes. Blend the cooked cauliflower, yoghurt, garlic rapeseed oil, Parmesan and salt until smooth.

2 portions

Creamy green vegetables

INGREDIENTS

- 1 courgette
- 100g spinach
- 3 celery sticks
- 1 leek
- 1/2 cabbage
- 100 ml double cream
- 1 tsp chilli powder
- Himalayan pink salt
- olive oil

INSTRUCTIONS

Slice the courgette and halve each slice. Shread the cabbage and slice the leek and the celery sticks.

Stir-fry the vegetables, including the spinach, in the olive oil until soft. This might take 5-10 minutes. Add the double cream and the seasoning and cook the vegetables for another 2 minutes. Serve with your favourite meat or with Halloumi.

2 portions

SNACKS

Cheesy biscuits

Chocolate peanut butter tipsy truffles

Peanut butter chocolate cookies

Spicy nuts

Kale crisps

"ELEVATE YOUR ENERGY WITH NOURISHING BITES THAT FUEL YOUR BODY AND MIND."

Cheesy biscuits

INGREDIENTS

- 200g almond flour
- 100g grated Cheddar
- 1 tsp baking powder
- 2tsp Chipotle Cayenne pepper
- 2 tsp garlic powder
- 2 tbsp Greek yoghurt
- 2 eggs

INSTRUCTIONS

Preheat the oven to 200°C. Choose the steam setting if possible. Mix all the ingredients. Spoon the mixture onto a large baking tray lined with baking paper. Bake the biscuits in the middle of the oven for 12 minutes.

To make the biscuits vegan, replace the cheese with dairy-free plant-based grated, the eggs with vegan egg replacer and the yoghurt with coconut double cream.

To make the biscuits dog-friendly, leave out the garlic powder and Cayenne pepper.

15 biscuits

Chocolate peanut butter tipsy truffles

INGREDIENTS

- 150g peanut or almond butter
- 70g dark raspberry chocolate
- 30g almond flour
- 2 tbsp whisky
- 2 tbsp almond milk

INSTRUCTIONS

Stir the whisky and almond flour into the peanut butter. Let the mixture rest in the fridge for 20-30 minutes. Break the chocolate into pieces and place it in a heatproof bowl set over a cooking pot with simmering water. Add the almond milk and stir until the chocolate melts. Leave the chocolate to cool down completely. Using two teaspoons, create a ball-shaped peanut butter and dip it into the chocolate. Refrigerate until set, ideally overnight.

15 truffles

Peanut butter chocolate cookies

INGREDIENTS

- 200g almond flour
- 50g dark chocolate chips
- 1/3 tsp xantham gum
- 3 tbsp peanut butter
- 20 ml walnut oil
- 2 tbsp Stevia sweetener
- 1 egg

INSTRUCTIONS

Preheat the oven to 180°C. If available, set the oven to a steam setting. Mix all the ingredients, divide the dough into 15 pieces, and roll each into a disc. Bake in the middle of the oven for 10 minutes.

15 cookies

Spicy nuts

INGREDIENTS

- 350g mixed unsalted nuts
- 1 tsp Cayenne pepper
- 2tsp Harissa spice
- pink Himalayan pink salt
- 50 ml olive oil

INSTRUCTIONS

Preheat the oven to 200ºC. Stir the spices, salt and olive oil through the nuts. Roast the nuts in a shallow tray lined with baking paper for 5-10 minutes until golden.

10 portions

Kale crisps

INGREDIENTS

- 200g curly kale
- olive oil
- 1 tsp Cayenne pepper
- ground black pepper

INSTRUCTIONS

Preheat the oven to 150°C. Tear the kale into bite-size pieces and toss it with olive oil, Cayenne pepper and some ground black pepper. Roast slowly for 25 minutes.

2 portions

WEEKLY MEAL PLANNER

	BREAKFAST	LUNCH	DINNER
MON	p.14	p.19	p.38
TUE	p.9	p.23	p.57
WED	p.13	p.30	p.64
THUR	p.10	p.26	p.43
FRI	p.8	p.25	p.48
SAT	p.7	p.24	p.52
SUN	p.11	p.31	p.42

A – Z

Index

a

Avocado
Salad with sausage meatballs, parmesan and avocado 29
Chicken pasta salad 32
Pork patties with Brie and dry mushrooms 58

Almond
Mini pancakes with strawberry jam and honey-flavoured syrup 7
Cinnamon granola with blueberry yoghurt 9
Salad with goat cheese, blackberries and toasted almonds 22
Meatballs with cauliflower puree and mushroom sauce 36
Fish and chips 59
Strawberry fool 68
Blackberry chocolate chia pudding 68
Chocolate granola and berry traybake 70
Blueberry ice-cream 71
Peanut butter cheesecake 72
Chocolate peanut butter tipsy truffles 80
Cheesy biscuits 81
Peanut butter chocolate cookies 82

Aubergine
Lamb and cauliflower moussaka 56

b

Bacon
Cooked breakfast with celeriac rosti 11
Baked egg casserole with bacon and parmesan crisps 8
Mushroom soup with bacon and parmesan chip 16
Pumpkin soup with bacon croutons 18
Lettuce cup with bacon and cheese 30
Egg mayo 31
Pork chops with cheesy winter vegetables 39
Pork loin skewer 47
Roasted Brussels sprouts 75

Beef
Leftover roast meat tortilla wrap with basil cream cheese 23
Cabbage beef mince wraps 25
Pasta with meatballs and Pecorino 35
Meatballs with cauliflower puree and mushroom sauce 36
Beef hot pot with gherkins, pancetta and fried onion 41
Meatloaf with kohlrabi wedges 51

Brussel sprouts
Roasted Brussels sprouts 75

A – Z
Index

b

Butter
Mini pancakes 7
Cooked breakfast with celeriac rosti 11
Mushroom soup with bacon and parmesan chip 16
Peanut butter turkey strips with rainbow chard 27
Meatballs with cauliflower puree and mushroom sauce 36
Pork chops with cheesy winter vegetables 39
Beef hot pot with gherkins, pancetta and fried onion 41
Cauliflower sausage bake 42
Venison strips with squash puree 46
Roasted duck crown with swede mash and red wine dark chocolate sauce 49
Pork fillet in herb butter with celeriac fries 55
Lamb and cauliflower moussaka 56
Vegetable patties with turnip chips 62
Harissa tofu with broccoli puree and kale crisps 65
Strawberry fool 69
Chocolate and berry traybake 70
Peanut butter cheesecake 72

Berries
Mini pancakes 7
Cinnamon granola with blueberry yoghurt 9
Raspberry peanut butter chia pudding 10
Strawberry smoothie 13
Salad with goat cheese, blackberries and toasted almonds 22
Roasted pumpkin, black pudding and blackberries salad 28
Blackberry chocolate chia pudding 68
Strawberry fool 69
Chocolate and berry traybake 70
Blueberry ice-cream 71

Broccoli
Brocolli soup with pork scratchings 20
Naked turkey burger with coconut tenderstem broccoli 45
Pork chops with cheese biscuits crumble and purple sprouting broccoli 53
Vegetable patties with turnip chips 62
Harissa tofu with broccoli puree and kale crisps 65
Tenderstem broccoli with garlic breadcrumbs 74

A – Z
Index

C

Cabbage
Grilled chicken breast with kohlrabi and watermelon radish salad 24
Cabbage beef mince wraps 25
Creamy green vegetables 78

Cacao
Strawberry smoothie 13

Cauliflower
Meatballs with cauliflower puree and mushroom sauce 36
Cauliflower sausage bake 42
Cauliflower chorizo creamy bake 44
Lamb and cauliflower moussaka 56
Cauliflower rice with chorizo, mushrooms and chives 57
Paneer spicy cauliflower rice 64
Spicy cauliflower rice 76
Garlic cauliflower puree 77

Celeriac
Cooked breakfast with celeriac rosti 11
Mackerel fishcakes 26
Pork chops with cheesy winter vegetables 39
Beef hot pot with gherkins, pancetta and fried onion 41
Stir-fry pork bun with celeriac crisp 48
Pork fillet in herb butter with celeriac fries 55

Cheese
Baked egg casserole with bacon and parmesan crisps 8
Breakfast muffins 14
Mushroom soup with bacon and parmesan chip 16
Brocolli soup with pork scratchings 20
Salad with goat cheese, blackberries and toasted almonds 22
Grilled chicken breast with kohlrabi and watermelon radish salad 24
Mackerel fishcakes 26
Roasted pumpkin, black pudding and blackberries salad 28
Salad with sausage meatballs, parmesan and avocado 29
Lettuce cup with bacon and cheese 30
Chicken pasta salad 32
Pasta with meatballs and Pecorino 35
Pork chops with cheesy winter vegetables 39
Stuffed marrow with salmon and cream cheese 40
Cauliflower sausage bake 42
Meatloaf with kohlrabi wedges 51
Cheesy spicy pork loins 52
Pork chops with cheese biscuits crumble and purple sprouting broccoli 53
Pork fillet in herb butter with celeriac fries 55

A – Z Index

c
Cheese
Cauliflower rice with chorizo, mushrooms and chives 57
Pork patties with Brie and dry mushrooms 58
Pumpkin vegetable bake 61
Roasted Brussels sprouts 75
Garlic cauliflower puree 77
Cheesy biscuits 80

Chicken
Grilled chicken breast with kohlrabi and watermelon radish salad 24
Chicken pasta salad 32
Chicken stuffed with spicy tomato chorizo mascarpone 43

Chocolate
Roasted duck crown with swede mash and red wine dark chocolate sauce 49
Blackberry chocolate chia pudding 68
Chocolate and berry traybake 70
Chocolate peanut butter tipsy truffles 81
Peanut butter chocolate cookies 82

Chorizo
Spicy chorizo soup 19
Chicken stuffed with spicy tomato chorizo mascarpone 43
Cauliflower chorizo creamy bake 44
Cauliflower rice with chorizo, mushrooms and chives 57

Cinnamon
Cinnamon granola with blueberry yoghurt 9

Coconut
Pumpkin soup with bacon croutons 18
Cauliflower sausage bake 42
Naked turkey burger with coconut tenderstem broccoli 45
Fish and chips 59
Paneer spicy cauliflower rice 64
Harissa tofu with broccoli puree and kale crisps 65

d
Dairy
Cauliflower chorizo creamy bake 44
Venison strips with squash puree 46
Stir-fry pork bun with celeriac crisp 48
Roasted duck crown with swede mash and red wine dark chocolate sauce 49
Pork chops with cheese biscuits crumble and purple sprouting broccoli 53
Pork fillet in herb butter with celeriac fries 55
Lamb and cauliflower moussaka 56
Pumpkin vegetable bake 61
Harissa tofu with broccoli puree and kale crisps 65 puree and kale crisps 65
Strawberry fool 69
Chocolate and berry traybake 70

A – Z
Index

d Dairy
Blueberry ice-cream 71
Peanut butter cheesecake 72
Garlic cauliflower puree 77
Creamy green vegetables 78
Cheesy biscuits 80

Duck
Roasted duck crown with swede mash and red wine dark chocolate sauce 49

e Eggs
Mini pancakes 7
Baked egg casserole with bacon and parmesan crisps 8
Cooked breakfast with celeriac rosti 11
Breakfast muffins 14
Mackerel fishcakes 26
Salad with sausage meatballs, parmesan and avocado 29
Egg mayo 31
Pork chops with cheesy winter vegetables 39
Meatloaf with kohlrabi wedges 51
Pork patties with Brie and dry mushrooms 58
Vegetable patties with turnip chips 62
Cheesy biscuits 80
Peanut butter chocolate cookies 82

f Fish
Mackerel fishcakes 26
Fish and chips 59

h Halloumi
Vegetable patties with turnip chips 62

Harissa
Pasta with meatballs and Pecorino 35
Penne with pork loin and Harissa paste 38
Pork chops with cheese biscuits crumble and purple sprouting broccoli 53
Paneer spicy cauliflower rice 64
Harissa tofu with broccoli puree and kale crisps 65
Spicy nuts 83

k Kale
Harissa tofu with broccoli puree and kale crisps 65
Kale crisps 84

Kohlrabi
Spicy chorizo soup 19
Grilled chicken breast with kohlrabi and watermelon radish salad 24
Meatloaf with kohlrabi wedges 51
Fish and chips 59

A – Z
Index

k
Konjac
Pork meatballs stir-fry 50
Roasted peppers and tofu bake 66

l
Lamb
Lamb and cauliflower moussaka 56

Mayonnaise
Egg mayo 31
Chicken pasta salad 32

m
Mushrooms
Baked egg casserole with bacon and parmesan crisps 8
Cooked breakfast with celeriac rosti 11
Breakfast muffins 14
Peanut butter turkey strips with rainbow chard 27
Meatballs with cauliflower puree and mushroom sauce 36
Cauliflower sausage bake 42
Cauliflower chorizo creamy bake 44
Venison strips with squash puree 46
Cauliflower rice with chorizo, mushrooms and chives 57
Pork patties with Brie and dry mushrooms 58
Vegetable patties with turnip chips 62
Harissa tofu with broccoli puree and kale crisps 65

n
Nuts
Chicken pasta salad 32
Stuffed marrow with salmon and cream cheese 40
Vegetable patties with turnip chips 62
Spicy nuts 83

o
Olive oil
Breakfast muffins 14
Pumpkin soup with bacon croutons 18
Salad with goat cheese, blackberries and toasted almonds 22
Roasted pumpkin, black pudding and blackberries salad 28
Salad with sausage meatballs, parmesan and avocado 29
Lettuce cup with bacon and cheese 30
Chicken pasta salad 32
Pasta with meatballs and Pecorino 35
Penne with pork loin and Harissa paste 38
Pork chops with cheesy winter vegetables 39
Beef hot pot with gherkins, pancetta and fried onion 41
Stir-fry pork bun with celeriac crisp 48
Pork meatballs stir-fry 50
Meatloaf with kohlrabi wedges 51
Cheesy spicy pork loins 52
Pork chops with cheese biscuits crumble and purple sprouting broccoli 53

A - Z
Index

o

Olive oil
Pork fillet in herb butter with celeriac fries 55
Pork patties with Brie and dry mushrooms 58
Vegetable patties with turnip chips 62
Paneer spicy cauliflower rice 64
Harissa tofu with broccoli puree and kale crisps 65
Roasted peppers and tofu bake 66
Tenderstem broccoli with garlic breadcrumbs 74
Roasted Brussels sprouts 75
Spicy cauliflower rice 76
Creamy green vegetables 78
Spicy nuts 83
Kale crisps 84

Pasta
Chicken pasta salad 32
Pasta with meatballs and Pecorino 35
Penne with pork loin and Harissa paste 38

Paneer
Paneer spicy cauliflower rice 64

p

Peanut butter
Raspberry peanut butter chia pudding 10
Strawberry smoothie 13

Peanut butter
Peanut butter turkey strips with rainbow chard 27
Naked turkey burger with coconut tenderstem broccoli 45
Peanut butter cheesecake 72
Chocolate peanut butter tipsy truffles 81
Peanut butter chocolate cookies 82

Pork
Brocolli soup with pork scratchings 20
Penne with pork loin and Harissa paste 38
Pork chops with cheesy winter vegetables 39
Pork loin skewer 47
Stir-fry pork bun with celeriac crisp 48
Pork meatballs stir-fry 50
Cheesy spicy pork loins 52
Pork chops with cheese biscuits crumble and purple sprouting broccoli 53
Pork fillet in herb butter with celeriac fries 55
Pork patties with Brie and dry mushrooms 58

Pumpkin
Pumpkin soup with bacon croutons 18
Roasted pumpkin, black pudding and blackberries salad 28
Pumpkin vegetable bake 61

A – Z
Index

S

Salad
Salad with goat cheese, blackberries and toasted almonds 22
Mackerel fishcakes 26
Roasted pumpkin, black pudding and blackberries salad 28
Salad with sausage meatballs, parmesan and avocado 29
Pork patties with Brie and dry mushrooms 58

Salmon
Stuffed marrow with salmon and cream cheese 40

Sausages
Cooked breakfast with celeriac rosti 11
Breakfast muffins 14
Salad with sausage meatballs, parmesan and avocado 29
Cauliflower sausage bake 42

Seeds
Raspberry peanut butter chia pudding 10
Pumpkin soup with bacon croutons 18
Roasted pumpkin, black pudding and blackberries salad 28
Salad with sausage meatballs, parmesan and avocado 29
Lettuce cup with bacon and cheese 30

Seeds
Pork patties with Brie and dry mushrooms 58
Pumpkin vegetable bake 61
Blackberry chocolate chia pudding 68
Roasted Brussels sprouts 75

Soy
Cooked breakfast with celeriac rosti 11
Cabbage beef mince wraps 25
Pork meatballs stir-fry 50

Squash
Venison strips with squash puree 46

Stevia sweetener
Mini pancakes 7
Blackberry chocolate chia pudding 68
Strawberry fool 69
Chocolate and berry traybake 70
Blueberry ice-cream 71
Peanut butter cheesecake 72
Peanut butter chocolate cookies 82

Swede
Roasted duck crown with swede mash and red wine dark chocolate sauce 49

A – Z Index

t Tofu
Harissa tofu with broccoli puree and kale crisps 65
Roasted peppers and tofu bake 66

Turkey
Peanut butter turkey strips with rainbow chard 27
Naked turkey burger with coconut tenderstem broccoli 45

v Venison
Venison strips with squash puree 46

w Wine
Cauliflower chorizo creamy bake 44
Roasted duck crown with swede mash and red wine dark chocolate sauce 49
Cauliflower rice with chorizo, mushrooms and chives 57

Frequently Asked
QUESTIONS

How do I get started with this new diet?

To understand the principles of healthy eating and adopt a low-carbohydrate lifestyle, visit https://www.holisticlowcarbhealthcoach.co.uk.

Will I be able to sustain my weightloss forever?

Your new healthy habits will become sustainable by adapting to a low-carbohydrate lifestyle and sticking to it. Your taste will change, and you won't crave carbohydrates or anything sweet. You will be able to keep the weight off for good.

Do you offer one-to-one coaching?

Yes, I offer a Personalised weight loss health coaching programme to help you start your healthy journey and Get unstuck single coaching session for those who are already on a low-carbohydrate diet but have stopped losing weight.

Are you a qualified health coach?

Yes, I have a Level 5 Health coaching qualification and plenty of experience with a low-carbohydrate lifestyle.

Do you need help starting on your new health journey? Would you like to learn more about a low-carbohydrate lifestyle? Let's work together on your new healthy you!

Start your natural path to holistic wellness today.

https://www.holisticlowcarbhealthcoach.co.uk/

If you enjoy this cookbook, please consider leaving a review online.

Printed in Great Britain
by Amazon